# Kids in the Kitchen™
## The Library of Multicultural Cooking

# Food and Recipes of China

Theresa M. Beatty

The Rosen Publishing Group's
**PowerKids Press™**
New York

The recipes in this book are intended for a child to make together with an adult.
*Many thanks to Ruth Rosen and her test kitchen.*

Published in 1999 by The Rosen Publishing Group, Inc.
29 East 21st Street, New York, NY 10010

Copyright © 1999 by The Rosen Publishing Group, Inc.

First Edition

Book Design: Resa Listort

Photo Credits and Photo Illustrations: Cover photo by John Bentham; pp. 9, 13, 17, 21 by Christine Innamorato; p. 5 © Mike J. Howell/International Stock Photo; p. 7 © Josef Beck/FPG International; p. 8 by Ira Fox; p. 11 © Luca Tettoni/Viesti Associates Inc.; p. 12 © Cliff Hollenbeck/International Stock Photo; pp. 15, 16 © Tom O'Brien/International Stock Photo; pp. 16, 20 © John Novajosky; p. 18 © Floyd Holdman/International Stock Photo.

Beatty, Theresa M.
      Food and recipes of China / by Theresa M. Beatty.
          p.     cm. — (Kids in the kitchen : multicultural cooking)
      Includes index.
      Summary: Describes some of the foods enjoyed in China and provides recipes for several popular Chinese dishes.
      ISBN 0-8239-5222-3
      1. Cookery, Chinese. 2. Food habits—China—Juvenile literature. [1. Food habits—China. 2. Cookery—Chinese.] I. Title. II. Series: Beatty,
      Theresa M.  Kids in the kitchen.
      TX724.5.C5B43  1998
      641.5951—dc21                                                                                    98-11214
                                                                                                                CIP
                                                                                                              AC

Manufactured in the United States of America

# CONTENTS

1 China 5

2 Chinese Cuisine 6

3 Chinese Foods 8

☯ Recipe: Don Far Tong (Chicken Egg-Drop Soup with Scallions) 9

4 Meals in China 10

5 The Wok 12

☯ Recipe: Chow Fon (Fried Rice) 13

6 Beijing Style 15

7 Cantonese 16

☯ Recipe: Cantonese Sweet and Sour Pork 17

8 Szechuan 19

9 Food and Festivals 20

☯ Recipe: Baat Bo Fon (Rice Pudding) 21

10 Chinese Food in America 22

Glossary 23

Index 24

---

Abbreviations   cup = c.   pound = lb.   tablespoon = tbsp.   teaspoon = tsp.

kilo = kilogram   liter = l   milliliter = ml

# CHINA

China is one of the largest countries on Earth. It is part of the **continent** (KON-tih-nent) of Asia, which is near Russia and the Middle East. Many people are farmers in China. More rice and wheat are grown there than in any other country in the world.

More than 1 billion people live in China. That's one-fifth of all the people living in the entire world!

China's history goes back almost 4,000 years. It is one of the oldest **civilizations** (sih-vih-lih-ZAY-shunz) in the world.

◀ *More people live in China than in any other country in the world.*

# CHINESE CUISINE

Chinese food is known as one of the great **cuisines** (kwih-ZEENZ) of the world. Preparing it is considered a form of art. And, as in most countries, different regions of China have their own special styles of cooking.

The food of China can be very healthy too. The Chinese were the first to discover that cooking vegetables quickly in just a little bit of sauce or water helps keep in most of the **nutrients** (NOO-tree-ints) that make vegetables healthy for you.

*The way food is presented is part of the art of Chinese cuisine.* ▶

# CHINESE FOODS

Rice is a popular food in China. Most Chinese dishes are served with rice. The rice is steamed and then eaten with flavorful meat and vegetable dishes. Sometimes rice is fried with little bits of meat and vegetables for a tasty dish.

Water chestnuts, bamboo shoots, and ginger root are often used in Chinese dishes. And the most popular meat in China is pork.

Chinese cuisine is also known for its delicious soups and noodle dishes as well. Many people believe that noodles were created in China.

# Don Far Tong
## (Chicken Egg-Drop Soup with Scallions)

**You will need:**

4 c. *(1 l)* chicken
   broth

1 tbsp. *(15 ml)* corn
   starch

1 egg

3 tbsp. *(40 ml)*
   chopped scallions

## HOW TO DO IT:

- Bring chicken broth to a boil in a large pot over medium-high heat. Reduce heat to simmer.
- Beat the egg in a bowl with a fork until fluffy.
- Mix corn starch with a few drops of water and stir into the broth.
- Slowly pour the egg into the soup while stirring constantly.
- Cook for 2 minutes or until the egg is cooked and looks like bits of scrambled eggs.
- Add chopped scallions.

Serves 4

Always ask a grown-up to help you when using knives!
Always ask a grown-up to help you when using the stove or oven!

# MEALS IN CHINA

In other countries around the world, food is often eaten in **courses** (KOR-siz), or one dish at a time. In China all the foods are served at once except at certain **banquets** (BANK-wetz). Many Chinese people eat soup at the end of a meal. Desserts are served only for special occasions.

Instead of forks and knives, Chinese people use **chopsticks** (CHOP-stiks) to eat. Chopsticks are thin sticks made from a strong plant called bamboo. They are held in one hand and used to scoop up food from a bowl. It takes some practice, but knowing how to use chopsticks is a lot of fun!

All of the foods seen here can be eaten▼
using just a pair of chopsticks.

# THE WOK

One of the most important **utensils** (yoo-TEN-sulz) in Chinese cooking is the **wok** (WOK). This is a cooking pot that looks like a big metal bowl. A wok is used to **stir-fry** (STUR-fry) foods.

The Chinese use the wok to cook dishes containing meat, vegetables, and rice. To stir-fry in a wok, the meat is cooked first along with steamed rice. The vegetables are added during the last minutes of cooking along with the seasoning.

This is done so that the vegetables stay crisp and keep their bright color and healthful **vitamins** (VY-tuh-minz).

# Chow Fon (Fried Rice)

*If you don't have a wok, you can use a large skillet for this recipe.*

## You will need:

3 tbsp. *(40 ml)* peanut oil

4 c. *(1 l)* boiled rice, cold

1 tsp. *(5 ml)* salt

½ tsp. *(2 ml)* black pepper

½ a green pepper, chopped

½ c. *(125 ml)* sliced mushrooms

¼ c. *(50 ml)* sliced water chestnuts

½ c. *(125 ml)* bean sprouts

¼ c. *(50 ml)* chopped scallions

3 eggs, beaten

½ c. *(125 ml)* chopped parsley

## HOW TO DO IT:

- Heat oil in a wok or skillet over high heat.
- Add rice and fry until hot, stirring constantly.
- Stir in salt and pepper.
- Add green peppers, mushrooms, water chestnuts, bean sprouts, and scallions. Continue stirring.
- Push mixture to the sides of the wok or skillet, making an empty space in the center of rice mixture.
- Pour beaten eggs into the empty space. Let cook halfway through.
- Blend eggs into the rest of the rice mixture.
- Heat until eggs are fully cooked.
- Remove from heat. Sprinkle chopped parsley over each serving.

Serves 4–6

Always ask a grown-up to help you when using knives!
Always ask a grown-up to help you when using the stove or oven!

# BEIJING STYLE

The city of **Beijing** (bay-ZHING) is in the northern part of China and is the country's capital. For many years, Beijing, or **Peking** (PEE-king) as it is also known, was home to the **emperors** (EM-pur-urz) of China. Emperors wanted great food for their banquets, so the cuisine of the north had to be very special. Peking duck is just one of the famous meals cooked by the great chefs of northern China.

Since northern China doesn't get as much rain as other parts of China, rice is not grown there. The people of northern China eat mostly noodles, thin pancakes, and dumplings.

◄ *From the great size of the emperor's palace at Beijing, you can imagine how grand the emperors' banquets were.*

15

# CANTONESE

Many people have tasted an egg roll at least once. Egg rolls come from the port city of Canton, or Guangzhou, in the south of China. To people in the United States and other parts of the world, **Cantonese** (kan-tuh-NEEZ) food is the most familiar kind of Chinese food.

The people of Canton eat a lot of seafood, such as lobster, shrimp, squid, and oysters. This is because their city is very close to the South China Sea.

16

# Cantonese Sweet and Sour Pork

## You will need:

½ c. (125 ml) flour
½ tsp. (2 ml) salt
½ tsp.(2 ml) black
    pepper
1 lb. (.45 kilo) lean pork
    loin, cut into bite-sized
    pieces
3 tbsp. (40 ml) peanut or
    vegetable oil
2 green peppers, cut in
    large pieces
1 onion, sliced
1 carrot, sliced
½ c. (125 ml)
    pineapple chunks
¼ c. (50 ml) white
    vinegar
2 tbsp. (30 ml) soy sauce
½ c. (125 ml)
    pineapple juice
¼ c. (50 ml) brown sugar
2 tbsp. (30 ml)
    cornstarch
Few drops red food
    coloring

## HOW TO DO IT:

- Mix flour, salt, and pepper in a plastic bag. Add pork pieces. Shake bag well to coat each piece. Remove pork and throw away bag.
- Heat oil in a large frying pan. Brown pork pieces on all sides.
- Lower heat and cook for 20 minutes.
- Add peppers, onions, and carrots. Fry for 5 minutes.
- Stir in remaining ingredients. Cook until mixture is hot.
- Serve over cooked rice.

Serves 4–5

Always ask a grown-up to help you when using knives!
Always ask a grown-up to help you when using the stove or oven!

# SZECHUAN

The **Szechuan** (SESH-wahn) region of China is in the central part of the country. One of the most important rivers in the world, the **Yangtze** (yang-SEE), runs through here. The **climate** (KLY-mit) is hot and **humid** (HYOO-mid), which is perfect for growing rice.

Szechuan food is known for how spicy it is. At a restaurant, any dish that is listed as Szechuan style is going to be very hot.

Favorite Szechuan seasonings and spices include hot peppers, green onions, ginger, soy sauce, garlic, vinegar, and sesame oil.

*The Yangtze River stretches over 3,000 miles, or 5,000 kilometers, from the Kunlun Mountains to the East China Sea.*

19

# FOOD AND FESTIVALS

During the Mid-Autumn Festival in September, Chinese people all over the world celebrate the full moon and the coming of autumn. They eat sweet pastries called mooncakes, just as Chinese people have for almost 700 years. Families gather together and eat the cakes, which contain fruit, nuts, or other fillings.

The dinner on the night before the Chinese New Year is also very important. In northern China, dumplings are served for good luck. Another part of the meal might also include dried oysters and black seaweed strands.

# Baat Bo Fon (Rice Pudding)

Here's a delicious dessert. But remember, the Chinese save desserts for special occasions, so save this recipe for a special time.

## You will need:

¾ c. *(175 ml)* rice
1½ c. *(375 ml)* water
pinch of salt
4 c. *(1 l)* milk
½ c. *(125 ml)* sugar
½ tsp. *(2 ml)* vanilla
extract

## HOW TO DO IT:

- ☯ Combine the rice, water, and salt in a large pot. Heat until almost boiling, stirring often.
- ☯ Lower heat, cover pot, and simmer for 15 minutes or until most of the water is gone.
- ☯ Stir in the milk and the sugar. Cook uncovered for 30 to 40 minutes or until mixture is thick and creamy, stirring often.
- ☯ Stir in vanilla.
- ☯ Serve topped with sliced almonds, whipped cream, or a sprinkle of cinnamon.
Serves 6

Always ask a grown-up to help you when using knives!
Always ask a grown-up to help you when using the stove or oven!

# CHINESE FOOD IN AMERICA

Over the last 30 years as Chinese people have moved to the United States, they brought their food and styles of cooking with them. Over time these cooking styles changed because Chinese American people were unable to get certain ingredients in the new places they settled.

Some of the dishes created in this way include chop suey or chow mein. Neither one of these popular dishes is actually from China. Fortune cookies were also created by Chinese Americans.

Whether you like chow mein or chow fon, you and your family are sure to enjoy cooking and tasting the Chinese recipes in this book.

# GLOSSARY

**banquet** (BANK-wet)  A large meal eaten in honor of a holiday or special event.

**Beijing** (bay-ZHING)  The capital of China.

**Cantonese** (kan-tuh-NEEZ)  Having to do with the city in southern China called Canton.

**chopsticks** (CHOP-stiks)  Two very thin sticks used for eating.

**civilization** (sih-vih-lih-ZAY-shun)  The ways of living of a people.

**climate** (KLY-mit)  The weather conditions of a certain place.

**continent** (KON-tih-nent)  A very large area of land.

**course** (KORS)  One of a number of dishes that make up a whole meal.

**cuisine** (kwih-ZEEN)  A style of cooking.

**emperor** (EM-pur-ur)  The ruler of an empire or of several countries.

**humid** (HYOO-mid)  Damp or moist.

**nutrient** (NOO-tree-int)  Anything that a living thing needs for energy or to grow.

**Peking** (PEE-king)  Another name for the Chinese capital of Beijing.

**stir-fry** (STUR-fry)  A method of Chinese cooking in which ingredients are cooked very quickly over high heat in a wok.

**Szechuan** (SESH-wahn)  An area of central China known for its spicy cooking.

**utensil** (yoo-TEN-sul)  A kind of tool usually used in cooking or eating.

**vitamin** (VY-tuh-min)  A nutrient that helps your body fight illness and grow strong.

**wok** (WOK)  A large, metal, bowl-shaped skillet used for cooking food quickly.

**Yangtze** (yang-SEE)  The largest river in China.

# INDEX

**B**
bamboo, 10
banquets, 10, 15

**C**
Cantonese, 16
chefs, 15
Chinese New Year, 20
chopsticks, 10
civilization, 5
climate, 19
continent, 5
courses, 10
cuisine, 6, 8, 15

**D**
dessert, 10

**E**
emperors, 15

**H**
healthy, 6
humid, 19

**M**
meat, 8, 12
Mid-Autumn Festival, 20

**N**
nutrients, 6

**R**
restaurants, 19
rice, 5, 8, 12, 15, 19

**S**
spices, 19
stir-fry, 12
Szechuan, 19

**U**
utensils, 12

**V**
vegetables, 6, 8, 12
vitamins, 12

**W**
wheat, 5
wok, 12

**Y**
Yangtze River, 19